HIDE & SEEK

Suganya Sundar

BookLeaf Publishing

Presentation by *BookLeaf Publishing*

Web: www.bookleafpub.com

E-mail: info@bookleafpub.com

ISBN: 9789357440356

First edition 2023

Until Home

A superhuman fulcrum
with bulk luggage balanced.
A little before dawn
she set out
to catch a bus,
to take home stories.
She stood in front of
a signature art frame
lit museum style
by tea stall nearby,
The orchestra of crickets
played their riffs.
Darkness, a double-edged sword
comforting though
for a prey in hiding,
one by one came the predators.
Unlike from the wild,
that are orthodox;
around here, its uncharted.
Could be a pair of eyes;
Sugar coated words;
unsought after help.
A numbness travelled.
from the feet rooted,
up the waist stressed,

to the heart ached.
The sunrise,
Few rides about face,
loud hunger pangs,
At a perceived breaking point
emerged her bus, slowly,
she breathed a sigh of relief.
The bus, however,
was just a different place.
Until Home...
Until Home.

Selective Hypocrisy.

A small restaurant
near a hectic bus stop
served house special pizza
and a sought-after grape juice.
Rumors said it was wine.
With friends,
mind was a teetotaler.
It refused to taste.
But being a stranger
means a hall pass.
Curiosity that lurked,
crawled out and peeped,
order for a pizza and
grape juice placed.
The rumors were untrue.
still a teetotaler
But a selective hypocrite.

Dream came true.

What are the odds?
thought the introvert psyche-
laid in bed,
The lockdown news ringed
the wind chimes,
in the garden of life.
For the one who rejoiced inside
a perfect game kicked off,
with the doors shut
and windows open
like a bear in hibernation.
Hiding in a favorite spot
with no seeker to spot,
Oh! the dream did come true.

Celestial Dust.

5

Flip through vintage pages
The Tyndall effect reveals,
Antique cryptic dust.

Transformation.

Fat caterpillar
hiding in cocoon for game
nowhere to be found.

Past.

One by one they left-
unnoticed, overlooked, obscure.
Each day of the year.

Seek.

I wish upon
A scavenger-hunt.
Perhaps,
a dusky magical forest,
through
a perilous path,
lined with
white wood asters.
To collect
Honesty, from red cardinal flowers
that hummingbirds feed.
Generosity, from roots
of the great wide meadow.
Courage, from the wind
on the top of the cliff.
Compassion, from the pine needles
of the nests up the trees.
Humility, from the crystals
of the deep dark caves.
And
Patience, all along the way
from every inhale and exhale.

Poof!

Ticking second hand
Don't blink for sixty ticks, once!
1 Minute vanishes.

Fear.

Walking down the street
An independent gutsy wight
As long as the way is lit,
Even on a no moon night.
Until a street light flicker,
then a transformation occurs.
Spooky feelings creep in,
the fear comes out weeping.
Atheist in the light.
A theist once ill- lit.
Peering through the shadows,
A scary thing that swallows.
A battle commences inside,
Before taking the stride.
What if's and But's fight,
while glued under light.
Fear runs through vein,
Pleas chasing in vain.
with a creak everything stops,
a broken sweat drops.
Into the darkness I steer,
reasoning the entity could also fear.
"Excuse me" I utter,
And move on for better.

Love.

When the seeker is love,
In your brown nebula eyes
A good place to hide.

A 1000 piece puzzle.

The mind thought-
"What a waste of time"
But heart yearned,
to fix in no time.
The mind asked the puzzle box,
"Do these improve me?"
"It might in a way",
the box smiled at heart.
The chit chat then paused,
it was overwhelming to start.
"Pick all the corners!"
mind told to heart.
With mind on the destination,
And heart on the journey,
Small portions were solved.
Then no piece fit
A plateau, they hit.
The whole picture was there,
hidden in plain sight.
Just like the everyday life.
Like a Zen master on time-lapse
the box gave some advice-
Walk away!
Be patient!
Trial and error!

Don't win!
Don't lose!
But complete.
They would eventually fall into place.
But not at a breakneck pace.

Sardines.

Of late
she dreams of playing sardines.
Every night,
Someone finds her place.
A shiny unicorn
with rainbow hair.
Fairies of kinds
each one a night
with sparkly stories
of tinkered thingies.
Mermaids with cyan scales
sharing sea adventures.
A wish dragon in pink
granting wish at a blink.
A dear friend
who plays fair.
A well wisher
who wishes well.
Let the seekers keep coming,
Into the happy hiding.

A Secret.

Just within arm's reach
Deep under plain cloths and skin
Unrequited love.

A Hole.

A supposed to be great evening,
With fun people partying,
The sun setting into a pool,
The glasses clinking into a song,
The aromatherapy of flowers,
the appetizing sight of food,
All unenjoyable-
cause a stitch came undone.
A hole in the pants
Hidden from sight,
Exposed by fright.
Making conscious move around
straight to powder room
When waiting for the stall
impatience grew tall.
while checking the gap in mirror
came out of stall a peer.
the mirror parted in half-
one with the rags
one with the riches.
"The usual place?"
Asked a pleasant voice.
A nod, A wistful smile, replied.
"Happens" and a smile.
The hole bothered no more.

Hide and Seek.

Sun yelling out loud-
Ready or not here I come!
A lunar eclipse.

Paracosm.

A treehouse painted.
With young chartreuse leaves of vine.
A rich jasmine scent.

Locked.

An old, creased picture.
Hold invisible story.
Needs the grandma key.

Ahh!!

Five four three two one
I froze admiring the flowers.
And forgot to hide.